I0426193

Evaluation of the Sensitivity of Inventory and Monitoring National Parks to Nutrient Enrichment Effects from Atmospheric Nitrogen Deposition

Chihuahuan Desert Network (CHDN)

Natural Resource Report NPS/NRPC/ARD/NRR—2011/305

T. J. Sullivan
T. C. McDonnell
G. T. McPherson
S. D. Mackey
D. Moore

E&S Environmental Chemistry, Inc.
P.O. Box 609
Corvallis, OR 97339

February 2011

U.S. Department of the Interior
National Park Service
Natural Resource Program Center
Denver, Colorado

The National Park Service, Natural Resource Program Center publishes a range of reports that address natural resource topics of interest and applicability to a broad audience in the National Park Service and others in natural resource management, including scientists, conservation and environmental constituencies, and the public.

The Natural Resource Report Series is used to disseminate high-priority, current natural resource management information with managerial application. The series targets a general, diverse audience, and may contain NPS policy considerations or address sensitive issues of management applicability.

All manuscripts in the series receive the appropriate level of peer review to ensure that the information is scientifically credible, technically accurate, appropriately written for the intended audience, and designed and published in a professional manner.

This report received peer review by subject-matter experts who were not directly involved in the collection, analysis, or reporting of the data. Data in this report were collected and analyzed using methods based on established, peer-reviewed protocols and were analyzed and interpreted within the guidelines of the protocols.

Views, statements, findings, conclusions, recommendations, and data in this report do not necessarily reflect views and policies of the National Park Service, U.S. Department of the Interior. Mention of trade names or commercial products does not constitute endorsement or recommendation for use by the U.S. Government.

This report is available from Air Resources Division of the NPS (http://www.nature.nps.gov/air/Permits/ARIS/networks/n-sensitivity.cfm) and the Natural Resource Publications Management website (http://www.nature.nps.gov/publications/nrpm/).

Please cite this publication as:

Sullivan, T. J., T. C. McDonnell, G. T. McPherson, S. D. Mackey, and D. Moore. 2011. Evaluation of the sensitivity of inventory and monitoring national parks to nutrient enrichment effects from atmospheric nitrogen deposition: Chihuahuan Desert Network (CHDN). Natural Resource Report NPS/NRPC/ARD/NRR—2011/305. National Park Service, Denver, Colorado.

NPS 960/106645, February 2011

Chihuahuan Desert Network (CHDN)

National maps of atmospheric N emissions and deposition are provided in Maps A and B as context for subsequent network data presentations. Map A shows county level emissions of total N for the year 2002. Map B shows total N deposition, again for the year 2002.

There are three parks in the Chihuahuan Desert Network that are larger than 100 square miles: Big Bend (BIBE), Guadalupe Mountains (GUMO), and White Sands (WHSA). There are also three smaller parks: Amistad (AMIS), Carlsbad Caverns (CAVE), and Fort Davis (FODA). Vegetation is dominated by arid and semi-arid plant communities, which are thought to be sensitive to nutrient N enrichment.

Total N emissions, by county, are shown in Map C for lands in and surrounding the Chihuahuan Desert Network. County-level emissions within the network ranged from less than 1 ton per square mile to between 5 and 20 tons per square mile. In general, emissions were less than 5 tons per square mile through most of the network. Point source emissions of oxidized (nitrogen oxides, NO_x) and reduced (ammonia, NH_3) N are shown in Map D. There are many point sources of N emissions within the network, with most smaller than about 800 tons per year. The larger point sources are all sources of oxidized N, although there are also many smaller scattered sources of reduced N. The largest point sources within the general vicinity of this network tend to be located outside the network in Texas, Arizona, and northwestern New Mexico. Urban centers within the network and within a 300-mile buffer around the network are shown in Map E. The only large population center within the network is El Paso, although there are several large urban centers with the 300-mile buffer outside the network, including Dallas, San Antonio, Houston, and Phoenix.

Total N deposition in and around the network is shown in Map F. Included in this analysis are both wet and dry forms of N deposition and both the oxidized and reduced N species. Total N deposition within the network ranged from less than 2 kg N/ha/yr to as high as 5 to 10 kg N/ha/yr. Most of the land area within the network receives total N deposition in the range of 2 to 5 kg N/ha/yr.

Land cover in and around the network is shown in Map G. The predominant cover types within this network are generally shrubland, grassland/herbaceous, and forest. There are also scattered areas of row crops and barren lands.

Map H shows the distribution within the larger (larger than 100 square miles) parks that occur in this network of the five vegetation types thought to be most responsive to nutrient N enrichment effects (arctic, alpine, meadow, wetland, and arid and semi-arid). In general, the predominant sensitive vegetation type within these parks is arid and semi-arid land, which occupies the majority of parkland within this network.

Park lands requiring special protection against potential adverse impacts associated with nutrient N enrichment from atmospheric N deposition are shown in Map I. Also shown on Map I are all federal lands designated as wilderness, both lands managed by NPS and also lands managed by other federal agencies. The land designations used to identify this heightened protection included Class I designation under the CAAA and wilderness designation. Both Class I areas and designated wilderness occur in this network. BIBE and portions of GUMO and CAVE are Class I areas. Wilderness areas occur inside and outside the parks.

Network rankings are given in Figures A through C as the average ranking of the Pollutant Exposure, Ecosystem Sensitivity, and Park Protection metrics, respectively. Figure D shows the overall network Summary Risk ranking. In each figure, the rank for this particular network is highlighted to show its relative position compared with the ranks of the other 31 networks.

The Chihuahuan Desert Network ranks in the lowest quintile, among networks, in N Pollutant Exposure (Figure A). Nitrogen emissions and N deposition within the network are both very low. However, the network Ecosystem Sensitivity ranking is High, in the second highest quintile among networks (Figure B). This is because the vegetation in this network is mainly arid and semi-arid vegetation, which are among the vegetation types expected to be especially sensitive to nutrient enrichment effects from N deposition. This network ranks in the third quintile in Park Protection (Figure C), having moderate amounts of protected lands.

In combination, the network rankings for Pollutant Exposure, Ecosystem Sensitivity, and Park Protection yield an overall Network Risk ranking that is Low, in the second lowest quintile among all networks (Figure D). The overall level of concern for nutrient N enrichment effects on I&M parks within this network is considered Low, slightly below the median among all networks.

Similarly, park rankings are given in Figures E through H for the same metrics. In the case of the park rankings, we only show in the figures the parks that are larger than 100 square miles. Relative ranks for all parks, including the smaller parks, are given in Table A and Appendix B. As for the network ranking figures, the park ranking figures highlight those parks that occur in this network to show their relative position compared with parks in the other 31 networks. Note that the rankings shown in Figures E through H reflect the rank of a given park compared with all other parks, irrespective of size.

Table A. Relative rankings of individual I&M parks within the network for Pollutant Exposure, Ecosystem Sensitivity, Park Protection, and Summary Risk from atmospheric nutrient N enrichment.

	Relative Ranking of Individual Parks[1]			
I&M Parks[2] in Network	**Pollutant Exposure**	**Ecosystem Sensitivity**	**Park Protection**	**Summary Risk**
Amistad	Low	High	Moderate	Low
Big Bend	Very Low	Very High	Very High	Very High
Carlsbad Caverns	Low	Very High	Very High	Very High
Fort Davis	Very Low	Very High	Moderate	Very Low
Guadalupe Mountains	Low	Very High	Very High	Very High
White Sands	Very Low	High	Moderate	Very Low

[1] Relative park rankings are designated according to quintile ranking, among all I&M Parks, from the lowest quintile (very low risk) to the highest quintile (very high risk).

[2] Park name is printed in bold italic for parks larger than 100 square miles.

The six parks in this network are all ranked Low to Very Low in Pollutant Exposure (Table A, Figure E). In contrast, park-specific Ecosystem Sensitivity rankings are much higher (Figure F, Table A). Individual parks are ranked in the highest (BIBE, CAVE, FODA, GUMO) or second highest (AMIS, WHSA) quintile in Ecosystem Sensitivity due to the presence of vegetation types expected to be highly sensitive to N enrichment. Park Protection is variable, with BIBE, CAVE, and GUMO ranked Very High, and other parks ranked Moderate (Figure G, Table A). The Summary Park Risk ranking is also variable, with AMIS, FODA and WHSA at the low end of the spectrum and BIBE, CAVE, and GUMO all ranked Very High (Figure H, Table A).

Map A. National map of total N emissions by county for the year 2002. Both oxidized (nitrogen oxides, NO_x) and reduced (ammonia, NH_3) forms of N are included. The total is expressed in tons per square mile per year. (Source of data: EPA National Emissions Inventory, http://www.epa.gov/ttn/chief/net/2002inventory.html)

Map B. Total N deposition for the conterminous United States for the year 2002, expressed in units of kilograms of N deposited from the atmosphere to the earth surface per hectare per year. Wet and dry forms of both oxidized (nitrogen oxides, NO_x) and reduced (ammonia, NH_3) N are included. For the eastern half of the country, wet deposition values were derived from interpolated measured values from NADP (three-year average centered on 2002) and dry deposition values were derived from 12-km CMAQ model projections for 2002. For the western half of the country, both wet and dry deposition values were derived from 36-km CMAQ model projections for 2002. NADP interpolations were performed using the approach of Grimm and Lynch (1997). CMAQ model projections were provided by Robin Dennis, U.S. EPA.

Map C. Total N emissions by county for lands surrounding the network, expressed as tons of N emitted into the atmosphere per square mile per year. The total includes both oxidized (nitrogen oxides, NO_x) and reduced (ammonia, NH_3) N. (Source of data: EPA National Emissions Inventory, http://www.epa.gov/ttn/chief/net/2002inventory.html)

Map D. Major point source emissions of oxidized (nitrogen oxides, NO_x) and reduced (ammonia, NH_3) N in and around the network. The base of each vertical bar is positioned in the map at the approximate location of the source. The height of the bar is proportional to the magnitude of the source. (Source of data: EPA National Emissions Inventory, http://www.epa.gov/ttn/chief/net/2002inventory.html)

Map E. Urban centers having more than 10,000 people within the network and within a 300-mile buffer around the perimeter of the network. (Source of data: U.S. Census 2000)

Map F. Total N deposition in and around the network. Included in the total are wet plus dry forms of both oxidized (nitrogen oxides, NO_x) and reduced (ammonia, NH_3) N. Values are expressed as kilograms of N deposited per hectare per year. (Source of data: CMAQ Model wet and dry deposition data for 2002; see information for Map B above for details)

Total Nitrogen Emissions by County Conterminous U.S.
(tons per sq. mi per year)

Total Nitrogen Emissions
(tons per sq. mi per year)
- Less than 1
- Greater than 1 and up to 5
- Greater than 5 and up to 20
- Greater than 20 and up to 50
- Greater than 50 and up to 100
- Greater than 100 and up to 618
- U.S. States
- NPS Networks
- I & M Parks

Data Source: National Emissions Inventory (EPA, 2002)
Projection: Lambert Conformal Conic, NAD 1983
Produced for: National Park Service, Air Resources Division, 2010
Prepared by: E&S Environmental Chemistry

Map A

CHDN-5

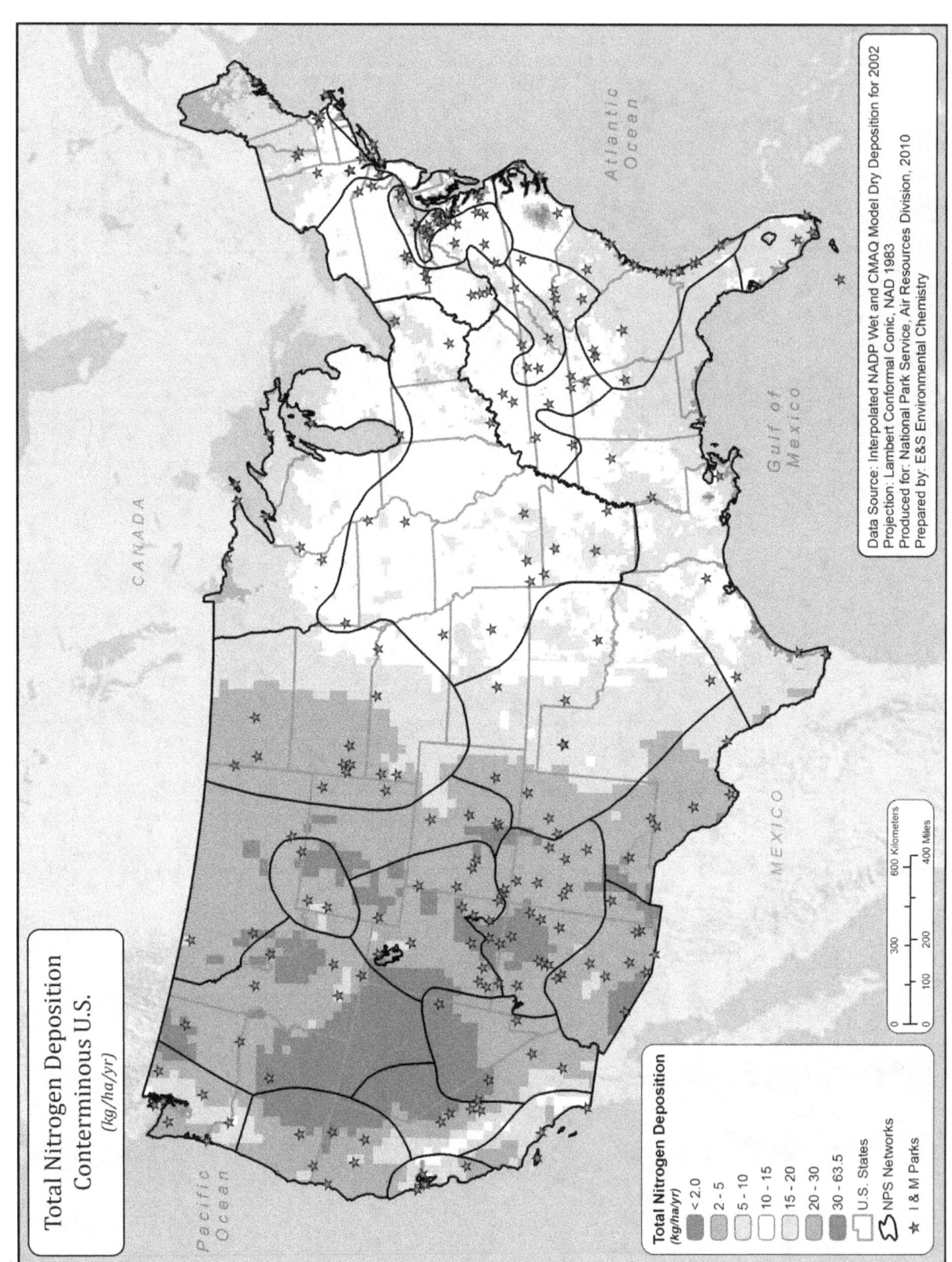

Total Nitrogen Deposition
Conterminous U.S.
(kg/ha/yr)

Total Nitrogen Deposition
(kg/ha/yr)
- < 2.0
- 2 - 5
- 5 - 10
- 10 - 15
- 15 - 20
- 20 - 30
- 30 - 63.5

U.S. States
NPS Networks
★ I & M Parks

Data Source: Interpolated NADP Wet and CMAQ Model Dry Deposition for 2002
Projection: Lambert Conformal Conic, NAD 1983
Produced for: National Park Service, Air Resources Division, 2010
Prepared by: E&S Environmental Chemistry

Map B

CHDN-6

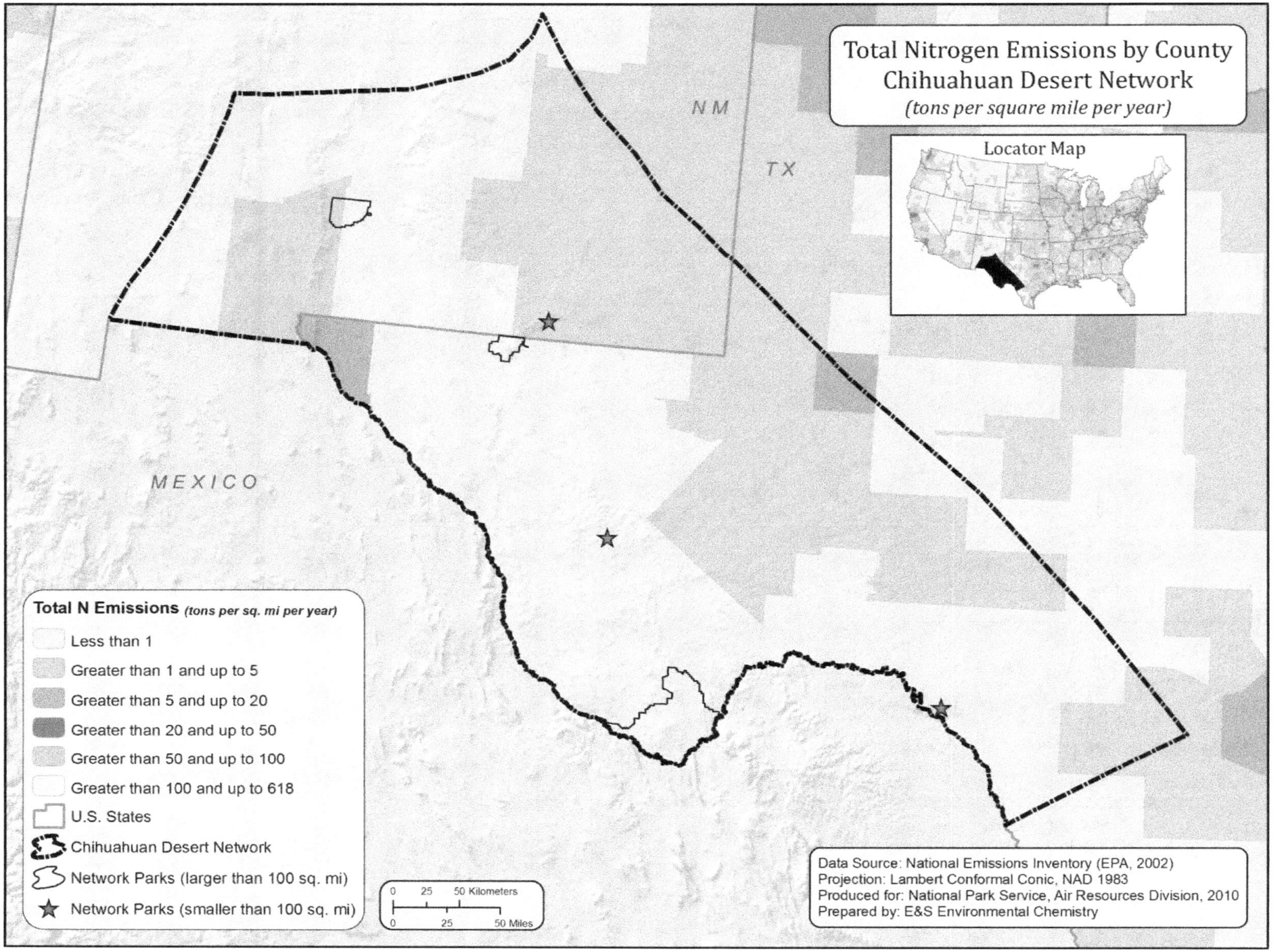

Total Nitrogen Emissions by County
Chihuahuan Desert Network
(tons per square mile per year)

Locator Map

NM

TX

MEXICO

Total N Emissions *(tons per sq. mi per year)*

Less than 1
Greater than 1 and up to 5
Greater than 5 and up to 20
Greater than 20 and up to 50
Greater than 50 and up to 100
Greater than 100 and up to 618
U.S. States
Chihuahuan Desert Network
Network Parks (larger than 100 sq. mi)
Network Parks (smaller than 100 sq. mi)

50 Kilometers
0   25   50 Miles

Data Source: National Emissions Inventory (EPA, 2002)
Projection: Lambert Conformal Conic, NAD 1983
Produced for: National Park Service, Air Resources Division, 2010
Prepared by: E&S Environmental Chemistry

Map C

CHDN-7

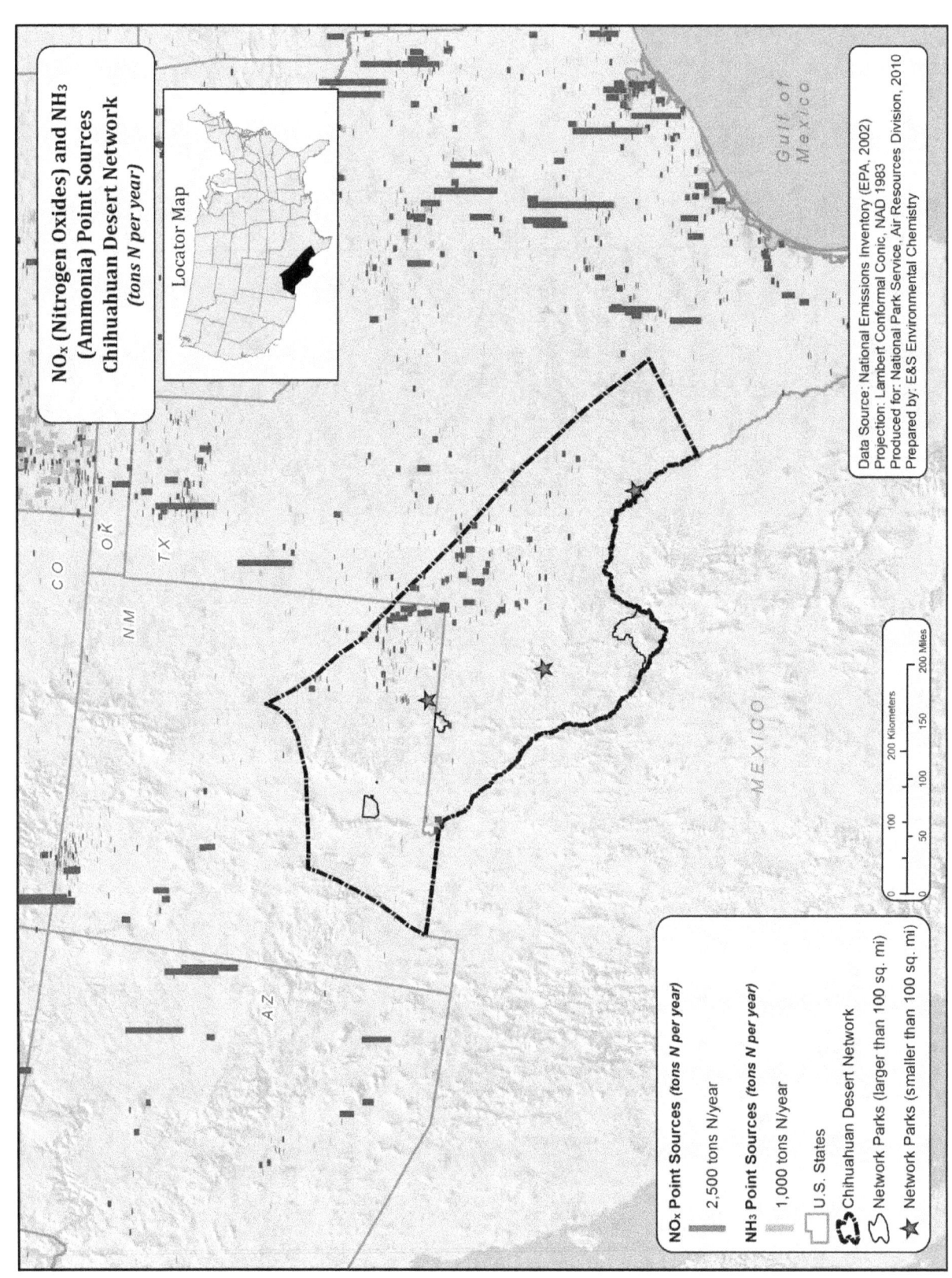

NOx (Nitrogen Oxides) and NH₃ (Ammonia) Point Sources Chihuahuan Desert Network
(tons N per year)

Locator Map

Gulf of Mexico

MEXICO

CO
OK
TX
NM
AZ

Data Source: National Emissions Inventory (EPA, 2002)
Projection: Lambert Conformal Conic, NAD 1983
Produced for: National Park Service, Air Resources Division, 2010
Prepared by: E&S Environmental Chemistry

NOx Point Sources *(tons N per year)*
2,500 tons N/year

NH₃ Point Sources *(tons N per year)*
1,000 tons N/year

U.S. States

Chihuahuan Desert Network

Network Parks (larger than 100 sq. mi)

Network Parks (smaller than 100 sq. mi)

0   50   100   150   200 Miles
0   100   200 Kilometers

Map D

CHDN-8

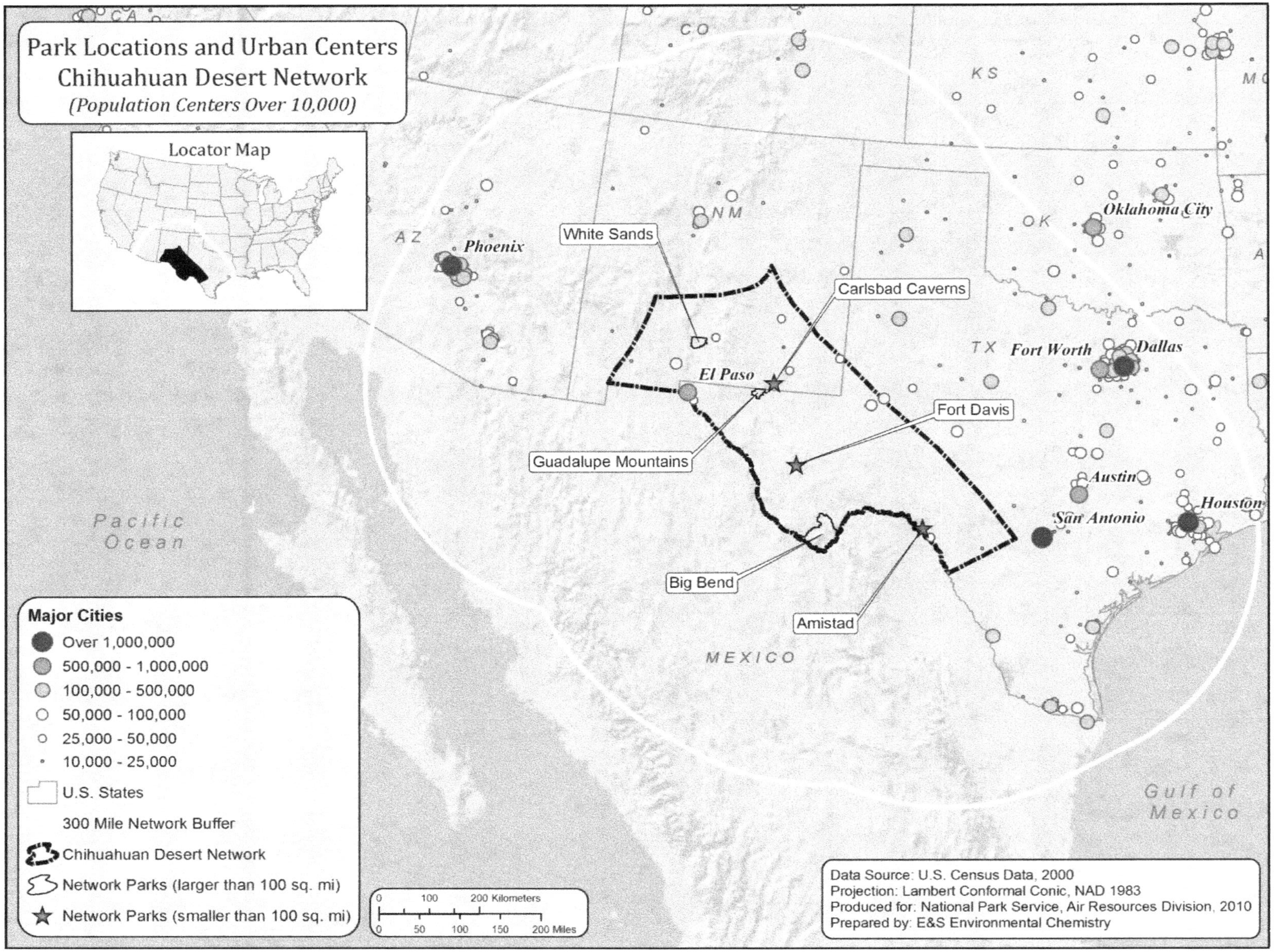

Park Locations and Urban Centers
Chihuahuan Desert Network
(Population Centers Over 10,000)
Locator Map
CA
CO
KS
AZ
NM
OK
TX
Phoenix
Oklahoma City
Fort Worth
Dallas
El Paso
Austin
San Antonio
Houston
White Sands
Carlsbad Caverns
Fort Davis
Guadalupe Mountains
Big Bend
Amistad
MEXICO
Pacific Ocean
Gulf of Mexico
Major Cities
Over 1,000,000
500,000 - 1,000,000
100,000 - 500,000
50,000 - 100,000
25,000 - 50,000
10,000 - 25,000
U.S. States
300 Mile Network Buffer
Chihuahuan Desert Network
Network Parks (larger than 100 sq. mi)
Network Parks (smaller than 100 sq. mi)
0 100 200 Kilometers
0 50 100 150 200 Miles
Data Source: U.S. Census Data, 2000
Projection: Lambert Conformal Conic, NAD 1983
Produced for: National Park Service, Air Resources Division, 2010
Prepared by: E&S Environmental Chemistry

Map E

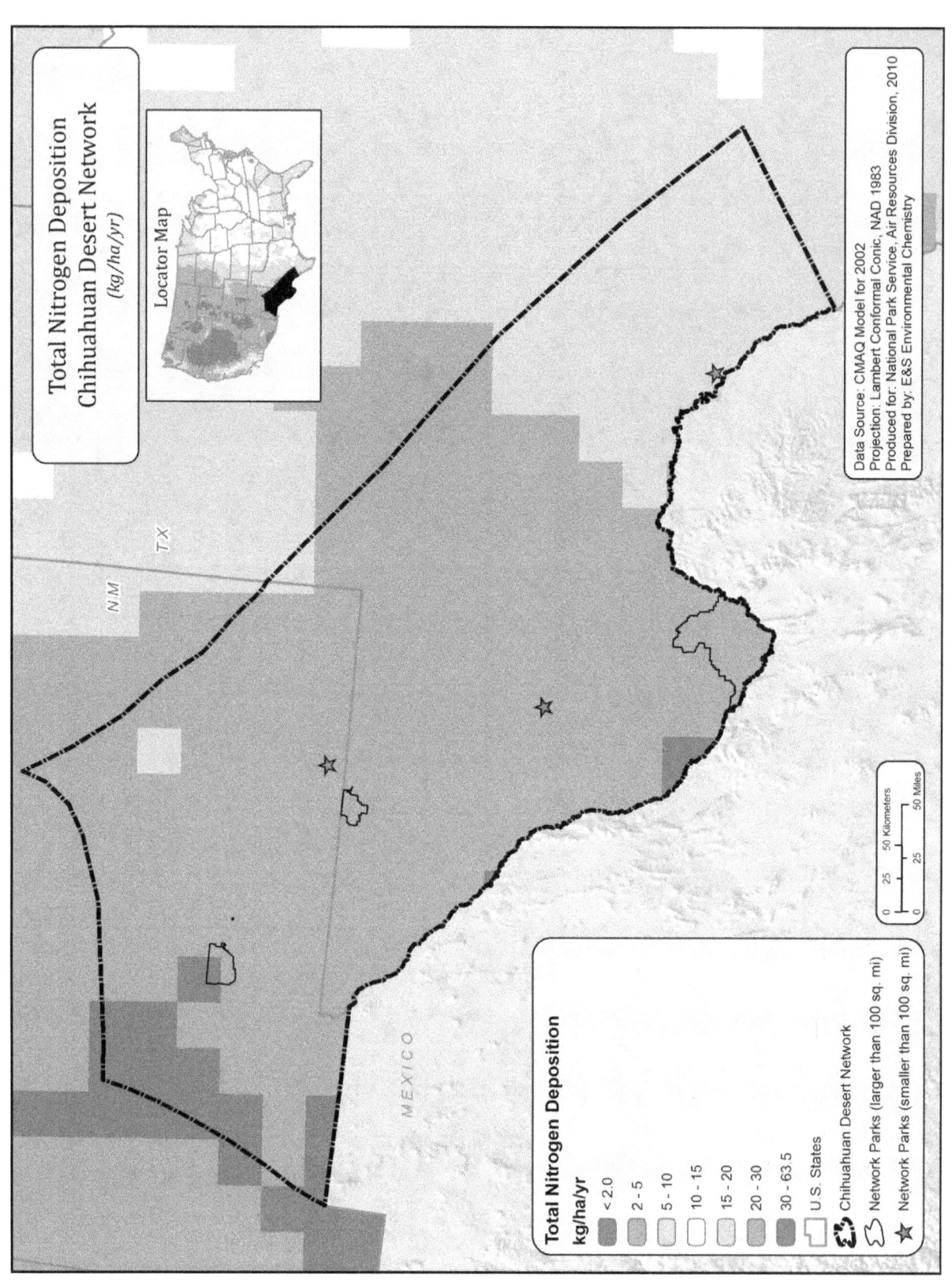

Total Nitrogen Deposition
Chihuahuan Desert Network
(kg/ha/yr)

Locator Map

N M

T X

MEXICO

Data Source: CMAQ Model for 2002
Projection: Lambert Conformal Conic, NAD 1983
Produced for: National Park Service, Air Resources Division, 2010
Prepared by: E&S Environmental Chemistry

Total Nitrogen Deposition
kg/ha/yr

- < 2.0
- 2 - 5
- 5 - 10
- 10 - 15
- 15 - 20
- 20 - 30
- 30 - 63.5
- U.S. States
- Chihuahuan Desert Network
- Network Parks (larger than 100 sq. mi)
- Network Parks (smaller than 100 sq. mi)

0   25   50 Kilometers
0   25   50 Miles

Map F

CHDN-10

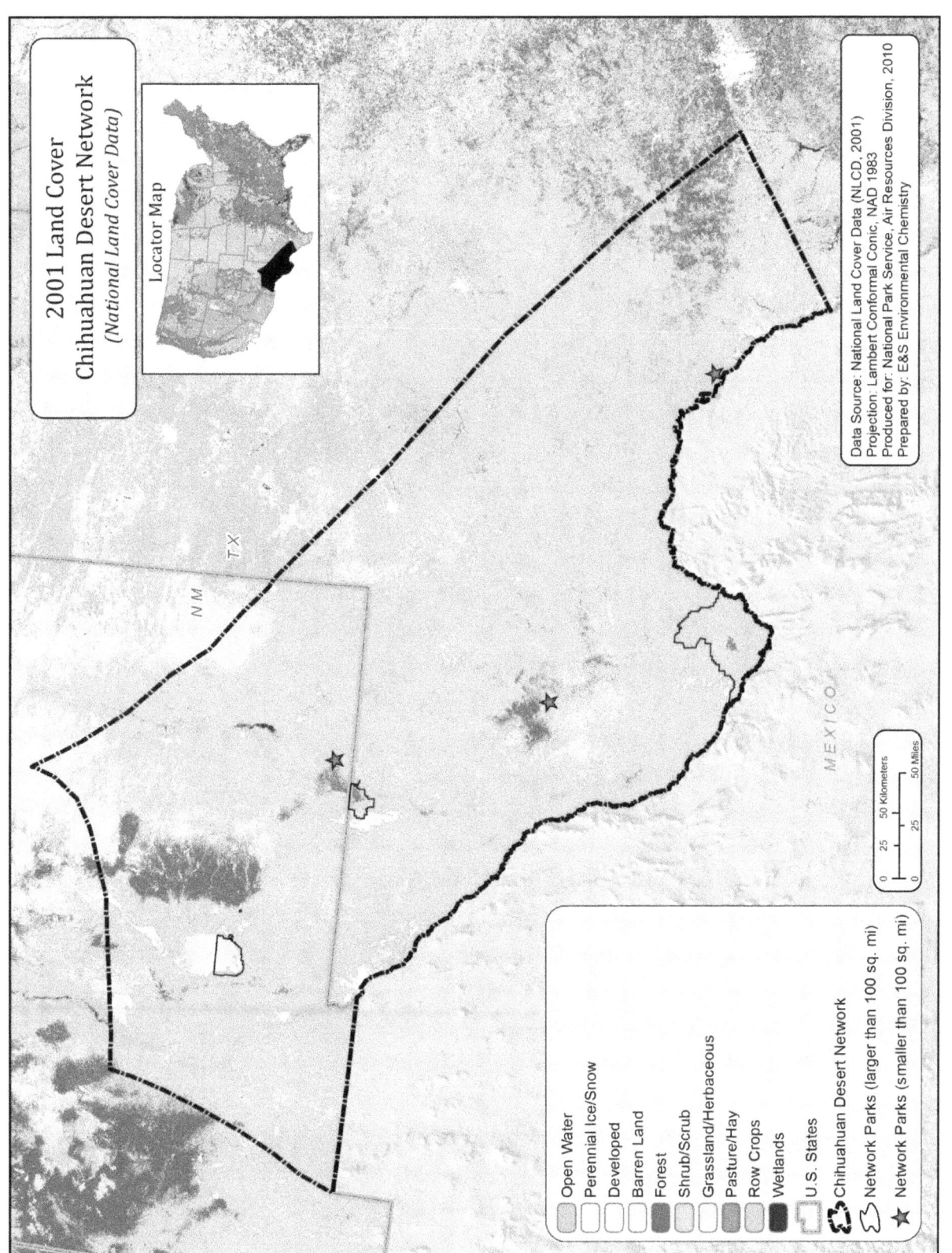

2001 Land Cover
Chihuahuan Desert Network
(National Land Cover Data)

Locator Map

Data Source: National Land Cover Data (NLCD, 2001)
Projection: Lambert Conformal Conic, NAD 1983
Produced for: National Park Service, Air Resources Division, 2010
Prepared by: E&S Environmental Chemistry

N M

T X

MEXICO

50 Kilometers
50 Miles
0   25
0   25

Open Water
Perennial Ice/Snow
Developed
Barren Land
Forest
Shrub/Scrub
Grassland/Herbaceous
Pasture/Hay
Row Crops
Wetlands
U.S. States
Chihuahuan Desert Network
Network Parks (larger than 100 sq. mi)
Network Parks (smaller than 100 sq. mi)

Map G

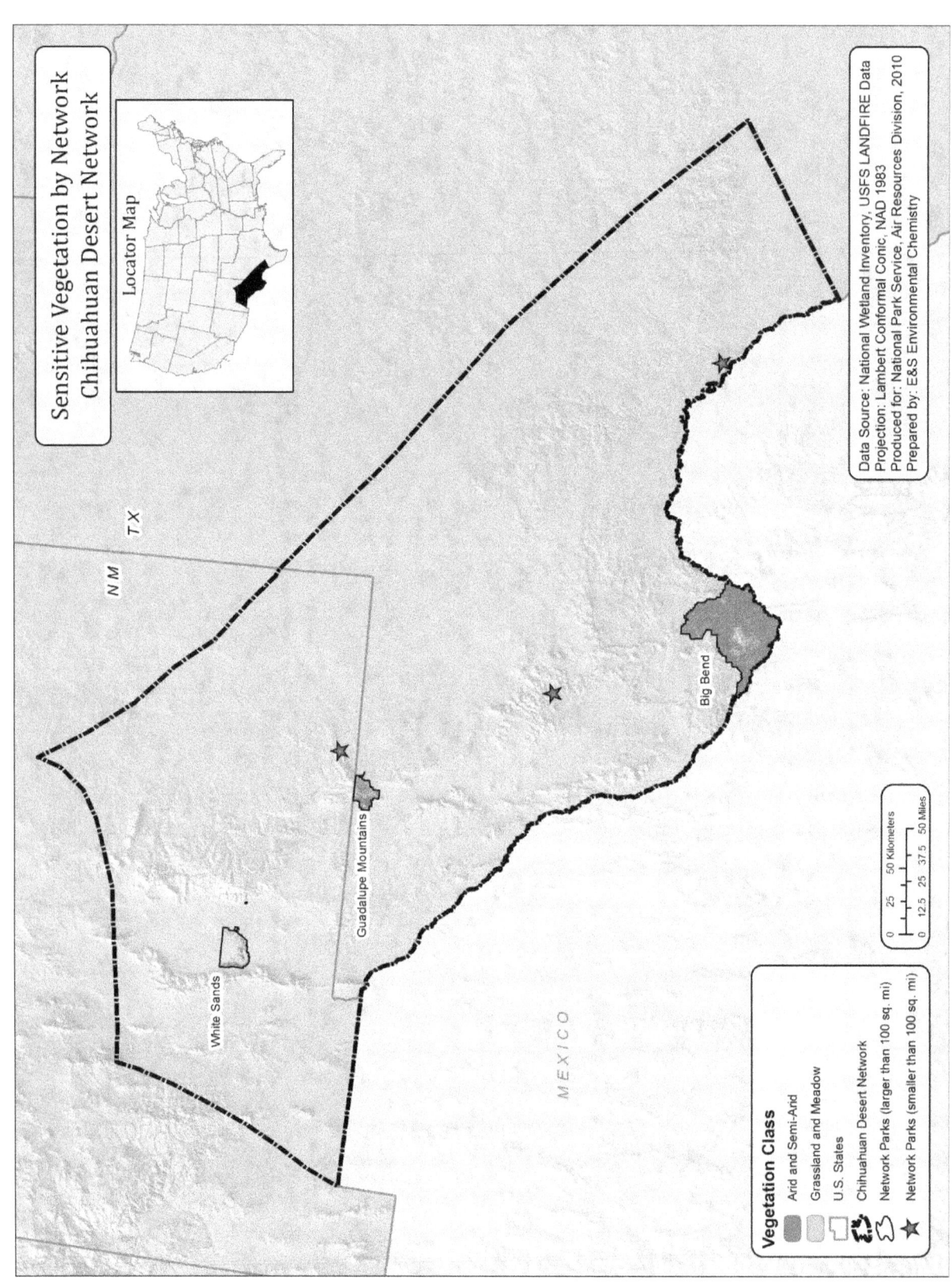

Sensitive Vegetation by Network
Chihuahuan Desert Network

Locator Map

Data Source: National Wetland Inventory, USFS LANDFIRE Data
Projection: Lambert Conformal Conic, NAD 1983
Produced for: National Park Service, Air Resources Division, 2010
Prepared by: E&S Environmental Chemistry

NM
TX

White Sands

Guadalupe Mountains

Big Bend

MEXICO

Vegetation Class

Arid and Semi-Arid
Grassland and Meadow
U.S. States
Chihuahuan Desert Network
Network Parks (larger than 100 sq. mi)
Network Parks (smaller than 100 sq. mi)

0   25   50 Kilometers
0   12.5   25   37.5   50 Miles

Map H

CHDN-12

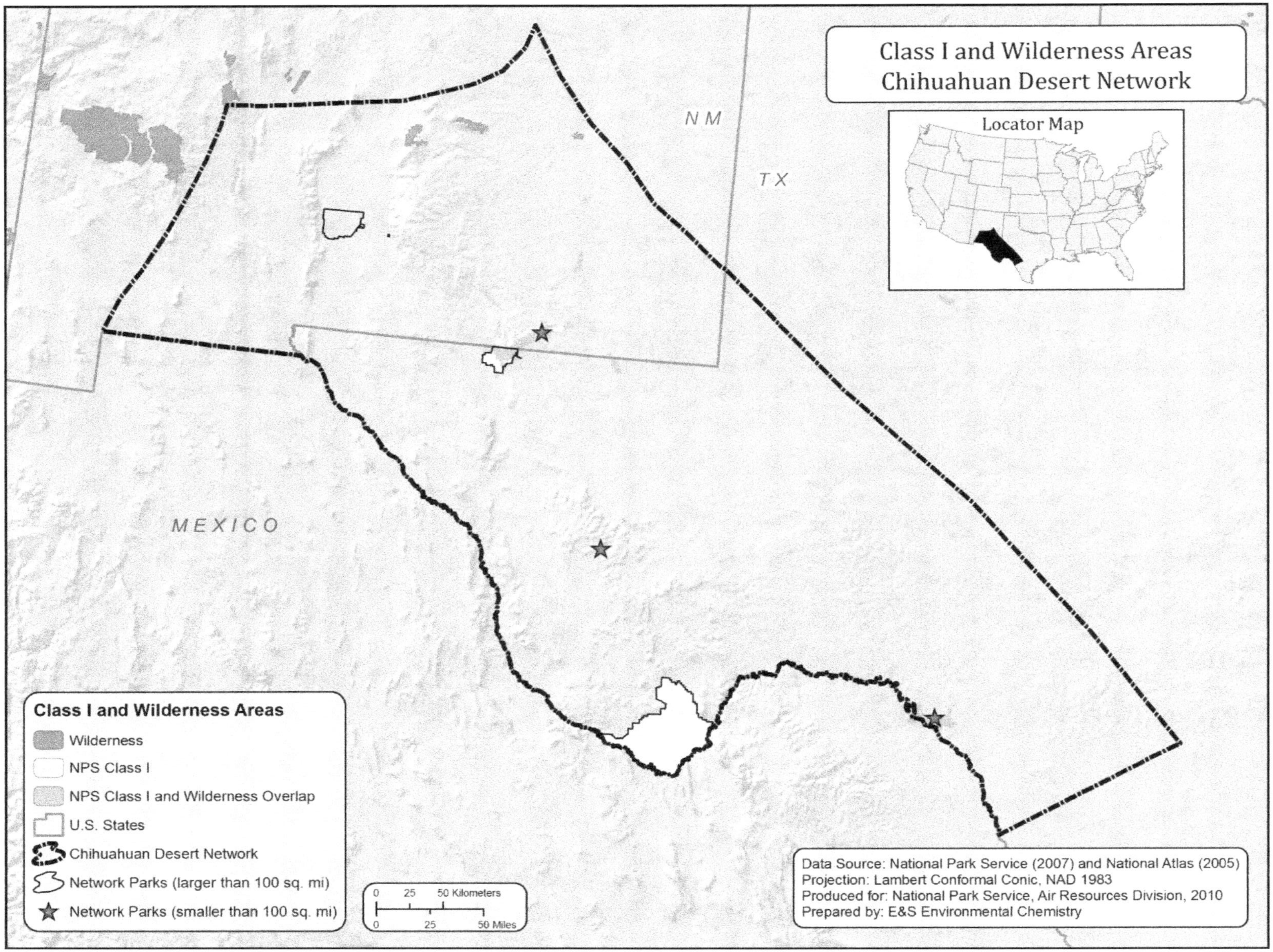

Class I and Wilderness Areas
Chihuahuan Desert Network

Locator Map

Data Source: National Park Service (2007) and National Atlas (2005)
Projection: Lambert Conformal Conic. NAD 1983
Produced for: National Park Service. Air Resources Division, 2010
Prepared by: E&S Environmental Chemistry

N M

T X

MEXICO

Class I and Wilderness Areas

Wilderness
NPS Class I
NPS Class I and Wilderness Overlap
U.S. States
Chihuahuan Desert Network
Network Parks (larger than 100 sq. mi)
Network Parks (smaller than 100 sq. mi)

0   25   50 Kilometers
0   25   50 Miles

Map I

CHDN-13

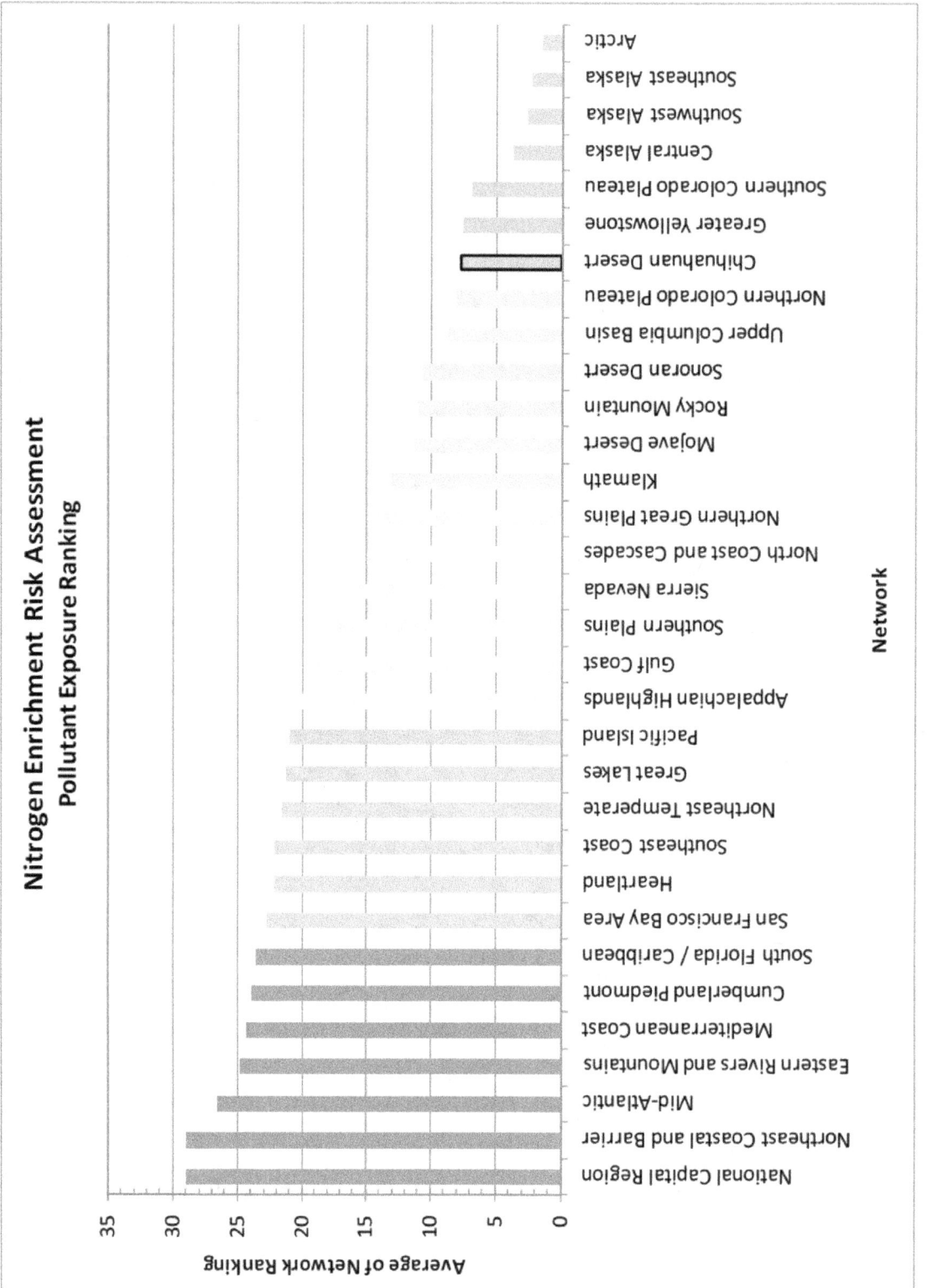

Figure A

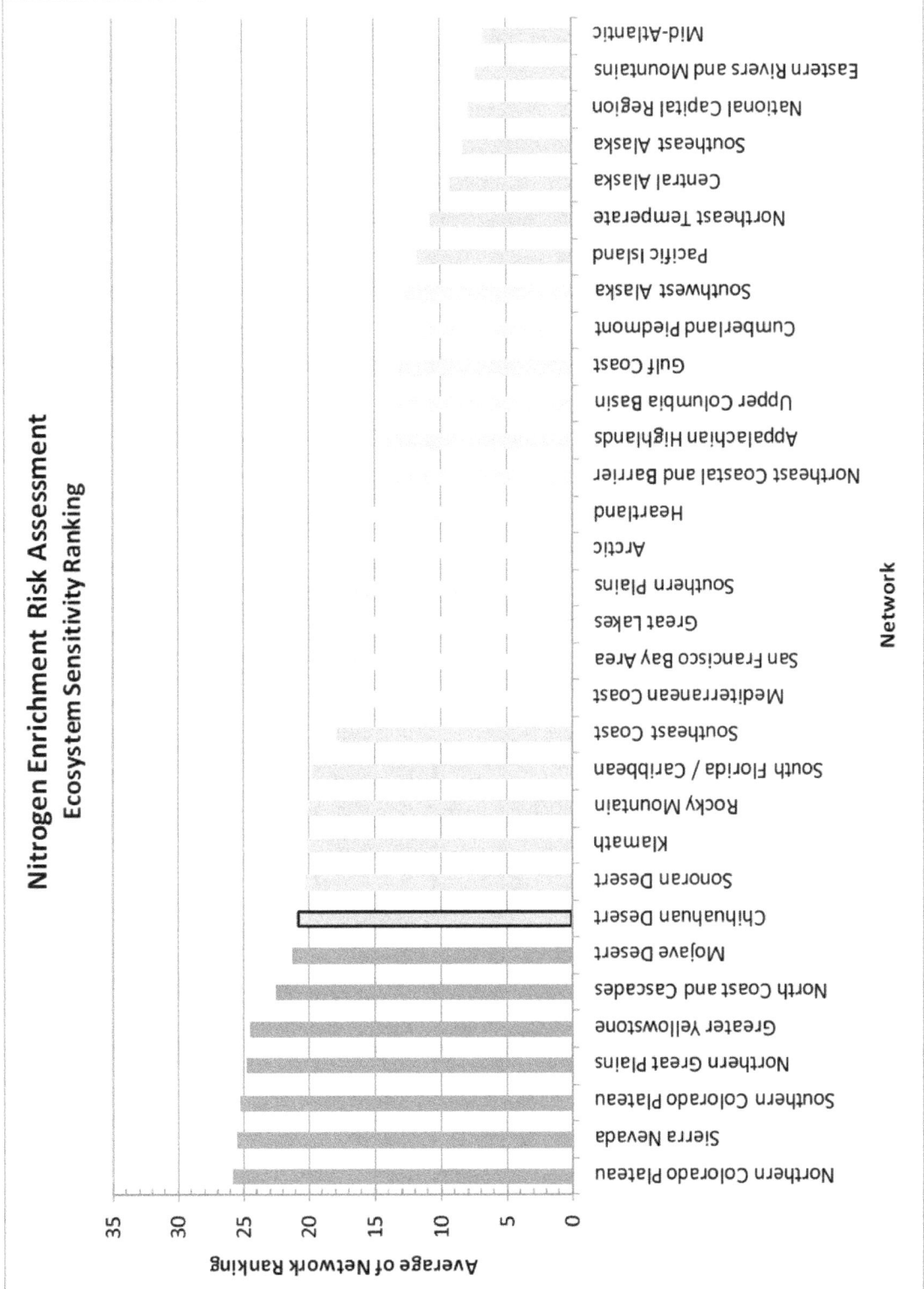

Figure B

CHDN-15

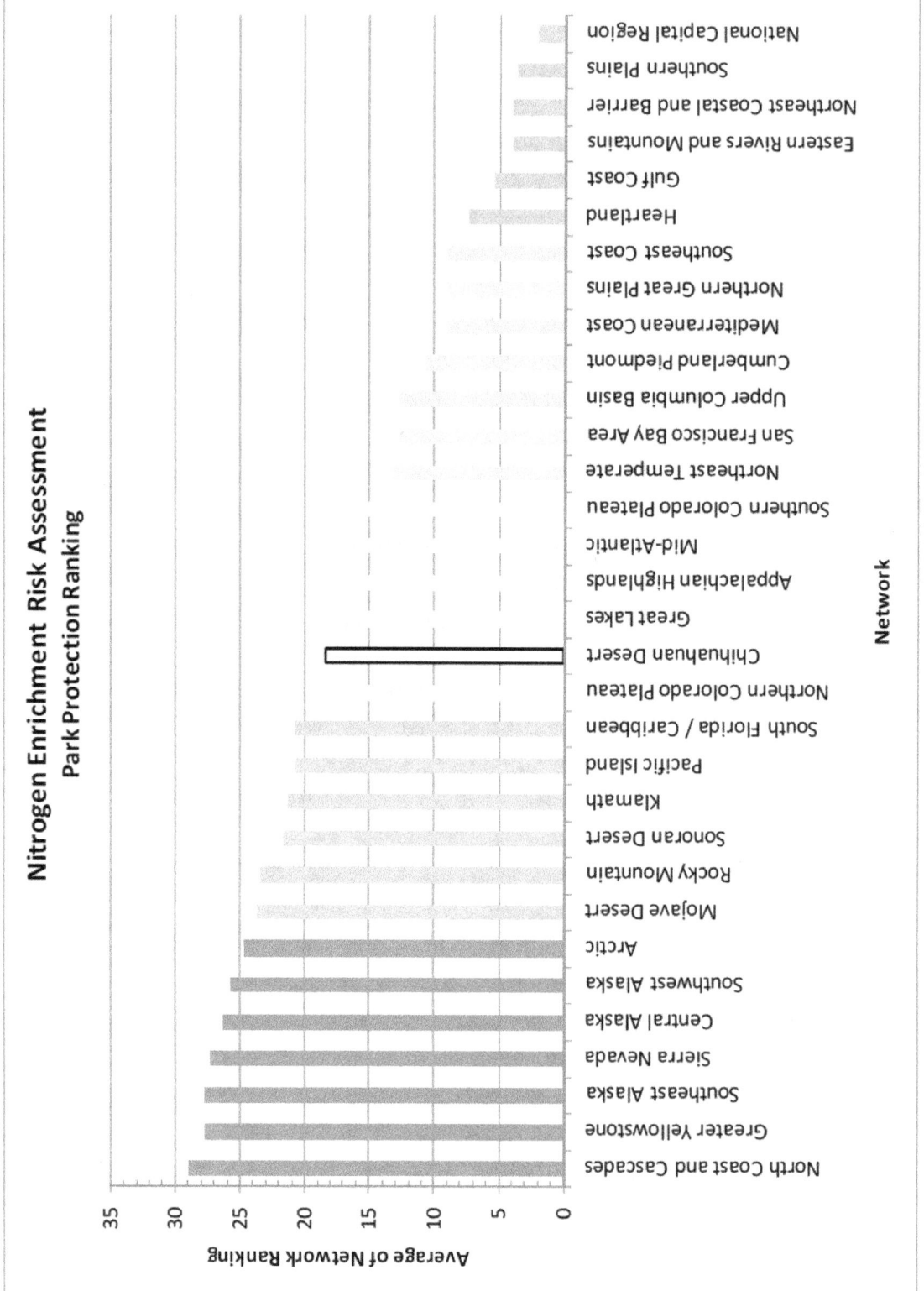

Figure C

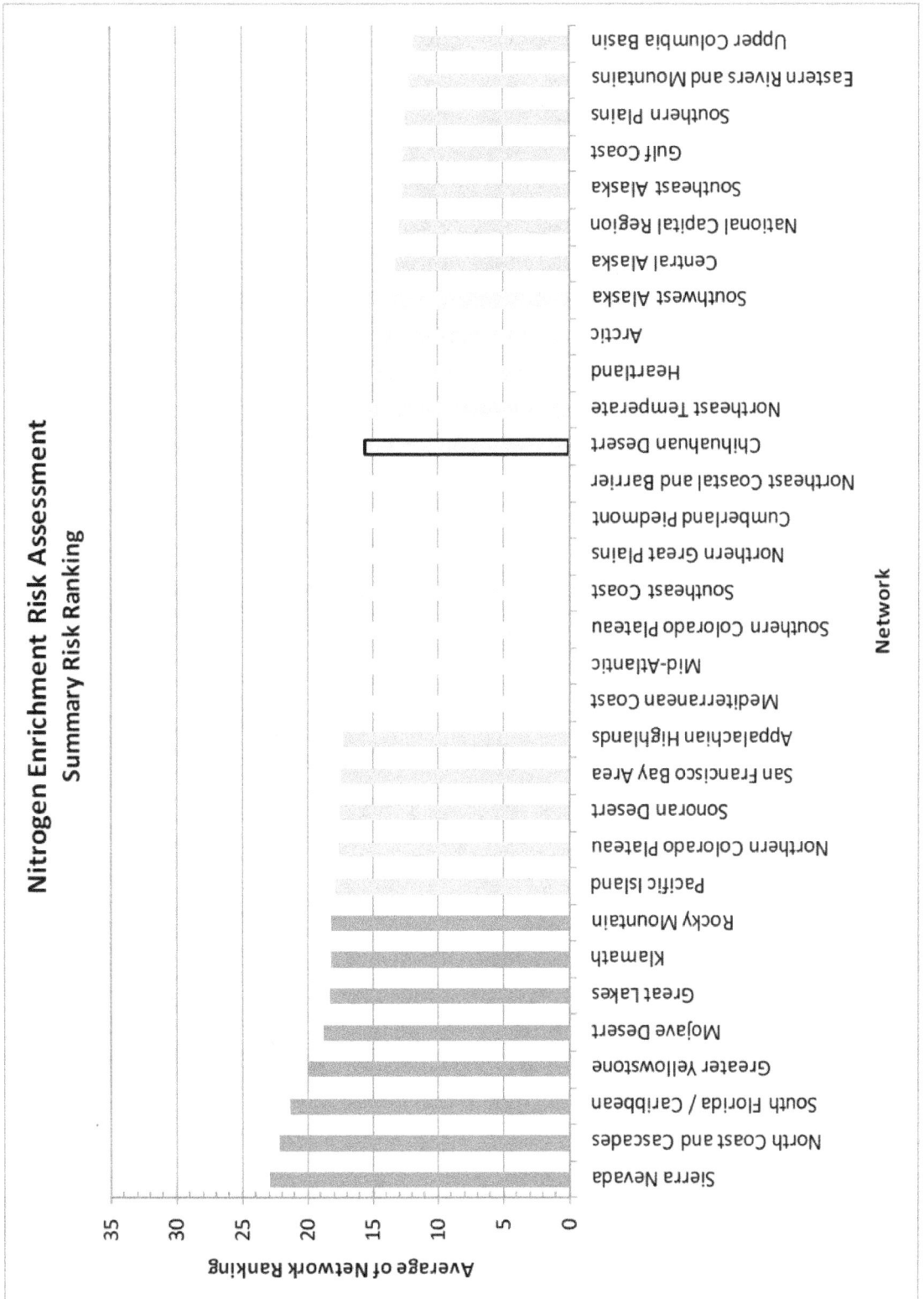

Figure D

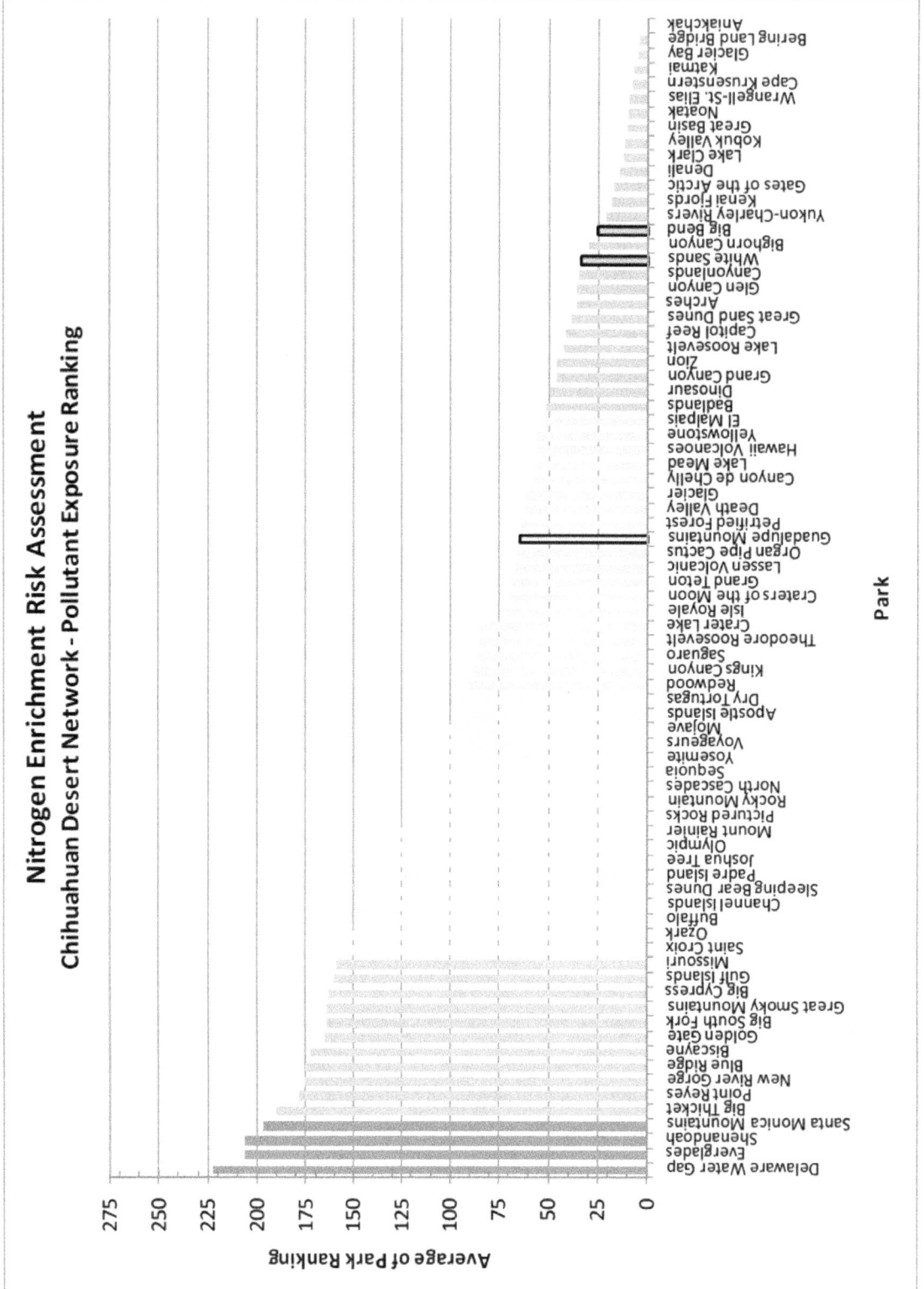

Figure E

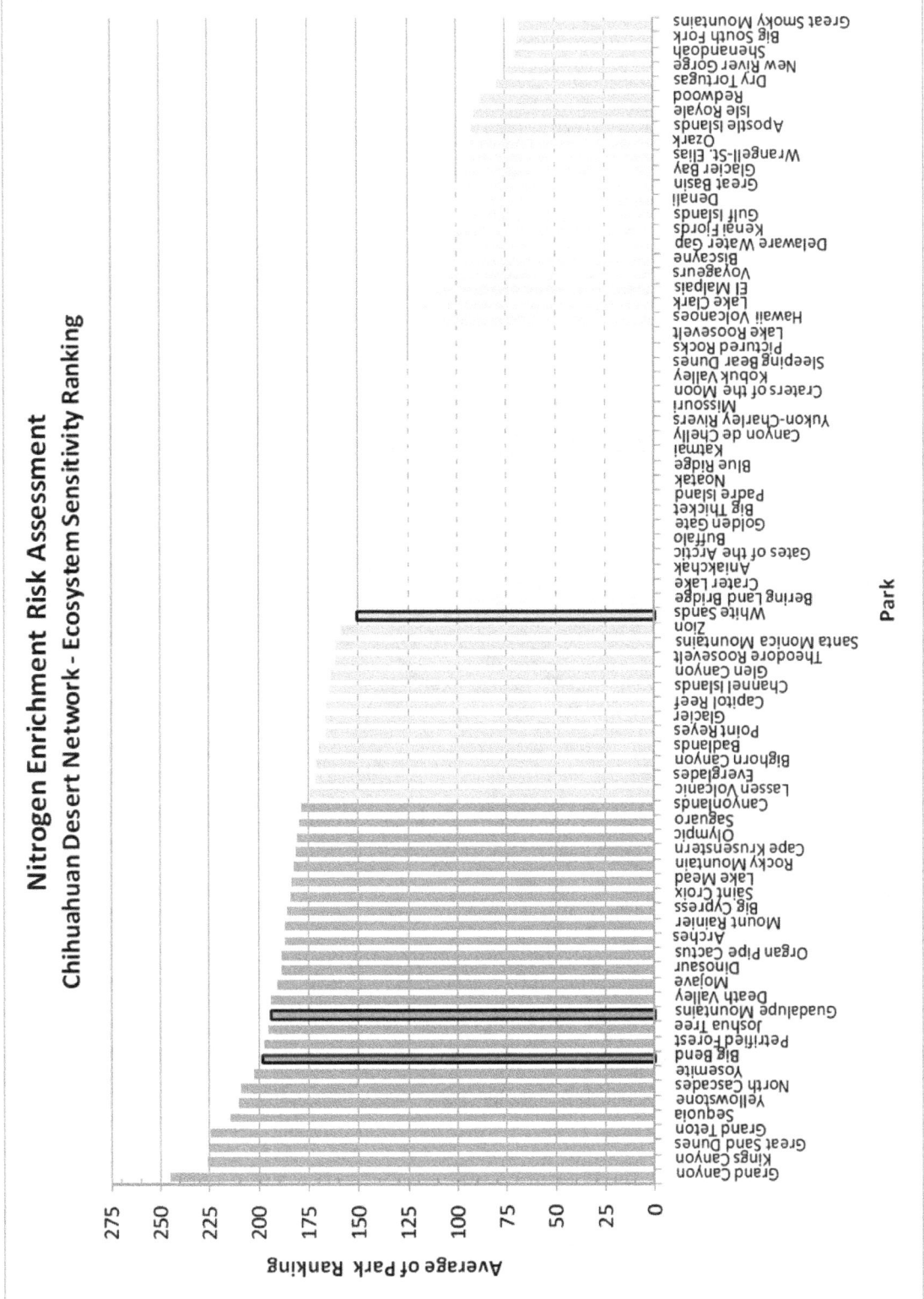

Figure F

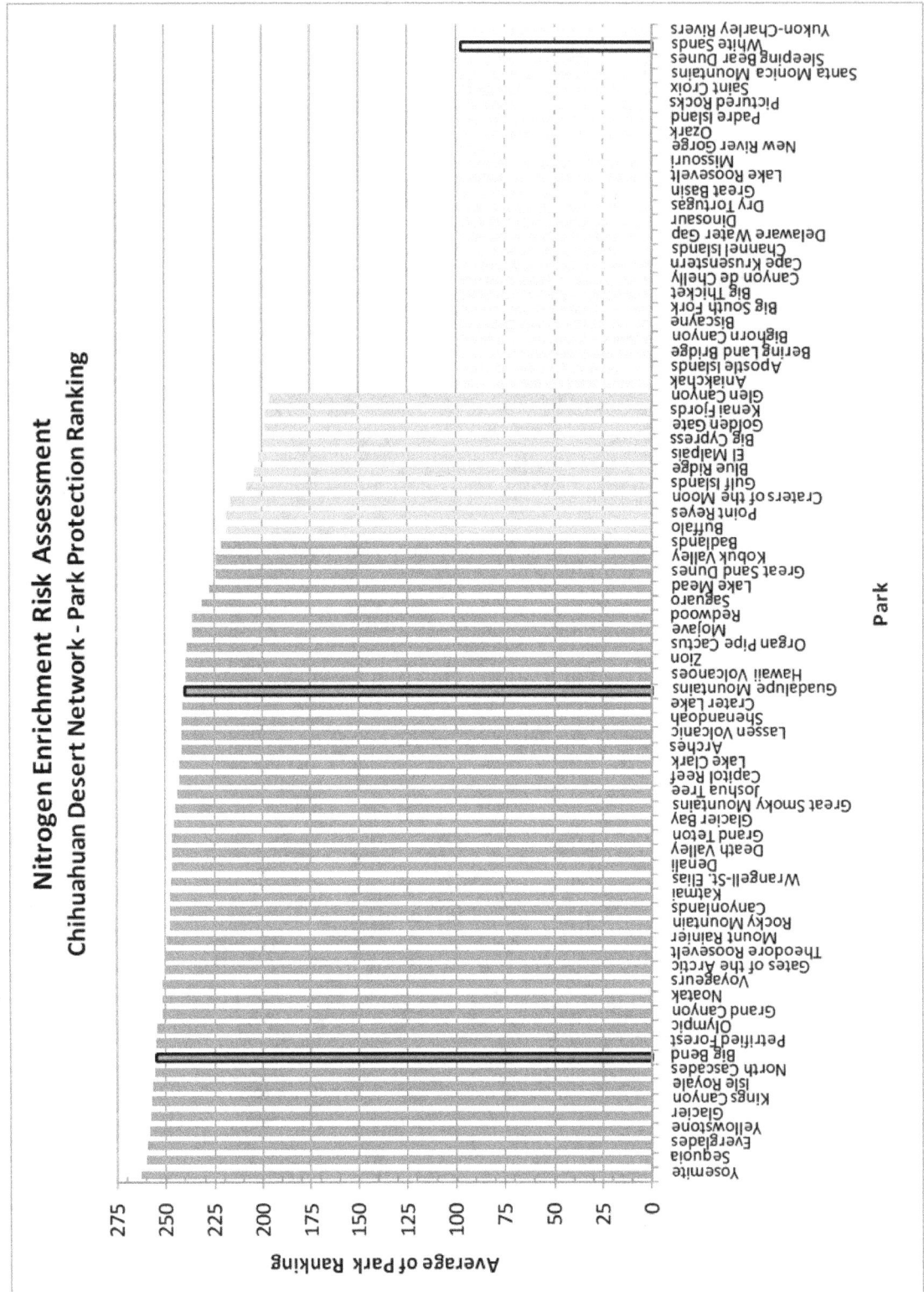

Figure G

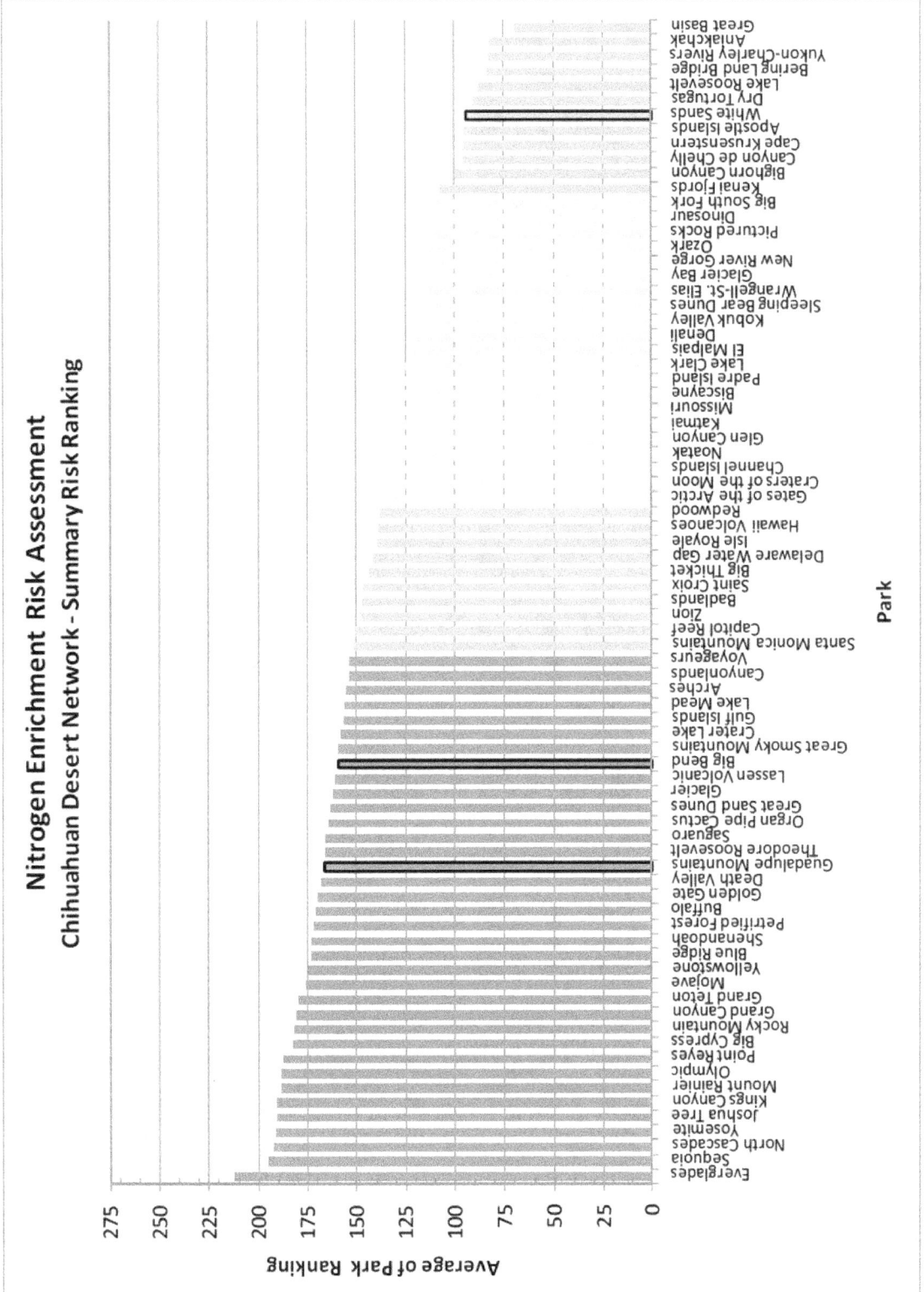

Figure H

The Department of the Interior protects and manages the nation's natural resources and cultural heritage; provides scientific and other information about those resources; and honors its special responsibilities to American Indians, Alaska Natives, and affiliated Island Communities.

NPS 960/106645, February 2011

www.ingramcontent.com/pod-product-compliance
Lightning Source LLC
Chambersburg PA
CBHW081152290526
45795CB00008B/2899